Listening
Comprehension
Lower

Activities to improve listening skills

Written by Graeme Beals
Published by Prim-Ed Publishing

The ability to listen with understanding is a major key to educational success. In fact, there is a very close correlation between listening ability and IQ scores.

The activities in *Listening Comprehension* are designed as teaching tools to build the listening skills of pupils. The activities are arranged to become progressively more difficult. It is expected that completion of two or three activities a week for approximately a month to six school weeks will gradually raise the listening vocabulary and concentration level of the pupils.

For each exercise, the teacher photocopies the accompanying picture sheet, allowing one sheet per pupil.

The activities can also be used as evaluative materials to identify problem areas and assess the development of pupils' listening skills. The graph sheet at the back of the book allows pupils to record each activity's results, providing immediate feedback on their listening skill development. It is suggested that the vocabulary difficulties pupils have also be recorded so these can be addressed in general teaching. Ensure the pupils know the exercises become a little harder so they do not feel unduly bad if their scores deteriorate slightly.

Contents

Exercise 1:   Lion 1

Exercise 2:   Bubbles 3

Exercise 3:   Skeleton 5

Exercise 4:   Honey Bear 7

Exercise 5:   Puppy 9

Exercise 6:   Snowman 11

Exercise 7:   Easter Bunny 13

Exercise 8:   Clown 15

Exercise 9:   Pirate 17

Exercise 10: Bath Time 19

Exercise 11: Food 21

Exercise 12: Sandcastle 23

Graph Sheet 25

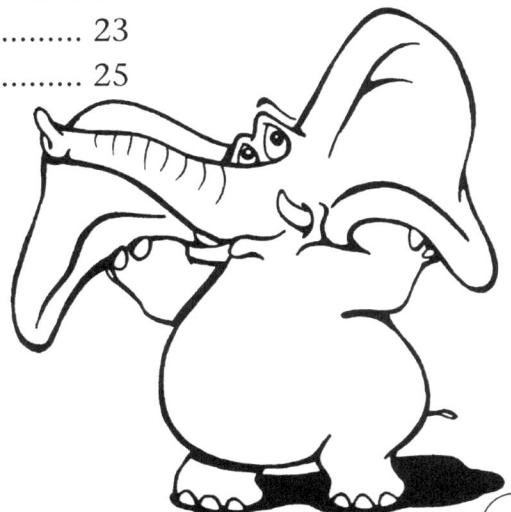

Prim-Ed Publishing

Each pupil has a copy of the picture and the appropriate coloured pencils or crayons.

The teacher reads out each of the instructions twice.

Allow time between each instruction for the pupils to complete the required task.

It does not matter greatly if pupils can see one another's papers, as there are instructions which require different responses from different pupils. You will quickly be able to establish which pupils are following others, and can then arrange to work with those pupils in future exercises.

Instructions

1. Write your name at the top of the page.

2. Colour the end of the lion's tail brown.

3. Put a circle around the lion.

4. Colour the lion's body yellow.

5. Give your lion some more teeth.

6. Colour the lion's hairy mane brown like his tail.

7. Find the piece in the drawing that shows that the lion is roaring and go over the lines in red.

8. Think of what the lion might have been eating for dinner and draw it on the ground behind the lion.

9. Colour the lion's eye in red.

10. If you would like to be this lion's dinner, put a line under your name, but if you would not like to be his dinner, put a line along the bottom of the page.

Prim-Ed Publishing

Listening Comprehension (Lower)

Each pupil has a copy of the picture and the appropriate coloured pencils or crayons.

The teacher reads out each of the instructions twice.

Allow time between each instruction for the pupils to complete the required task.

It does not matter greatly if pupils can see one another's papers, as there are instructions which require different responses from different pupils. You will quickly be able to establish which pupils are following others, and can then arrange to work with those pupils in future exercises.

Instructions

1. Write your name at the bottom of the page.

2. Colour the girl's hair ribbon red.

3. Put a circle around the smallest bubble.

4. Colour the biggest bubble blue.

5. Draw a bubble bigger than all the others.

6. Colour the bubble the girl is blowing green.

7. Find the freckles on the girl's face and go over them with yellow.

8. If the girl is blowing to make the bubbles, draw in a line to show where the air from her mouth must be going.

9. Colour the girl's hair orange.

10. If you think she uses water to make the bubbles, colour the smallest bubble blue, but if you think she uses dishwashing liquid, colour it green.

Prim-Ed Publishing

Each pupil has a copy of the picture and the appropriate coloured pencils or crayons.

The teacher reads out each of the instructions twice.

Allow time between each instruction for the pupils to complete the required task.

It does not matter greatly if pupils can see one another's papers, as there are instructions which require different responses from different pupils. You will quickly be able to establish which pupils are following others, and can then arrange to work with those pupils in future exercises.

Instructions

1. Write your name between the skeleton's hands.

2. Colour the skeleton's head red.

3. Put a circle around the skeleton's feet.

4. Colour the skeleton's arms green.

5. Draw a box between the skeleton's legs, for it to sit on.

6. Colour the skeleton's legs blue.

7. Find the skeleton's two knees and put a circle around each of them.

8. Think who the skeleton might be talking to and draw a stick-figure person next to the skeleton.

9. Colour the skeleton's ribs in brown.

10. If you think there is a skeleton inside you, put a line right around the edge of this page. If you think there isn't, just put a line under your name.

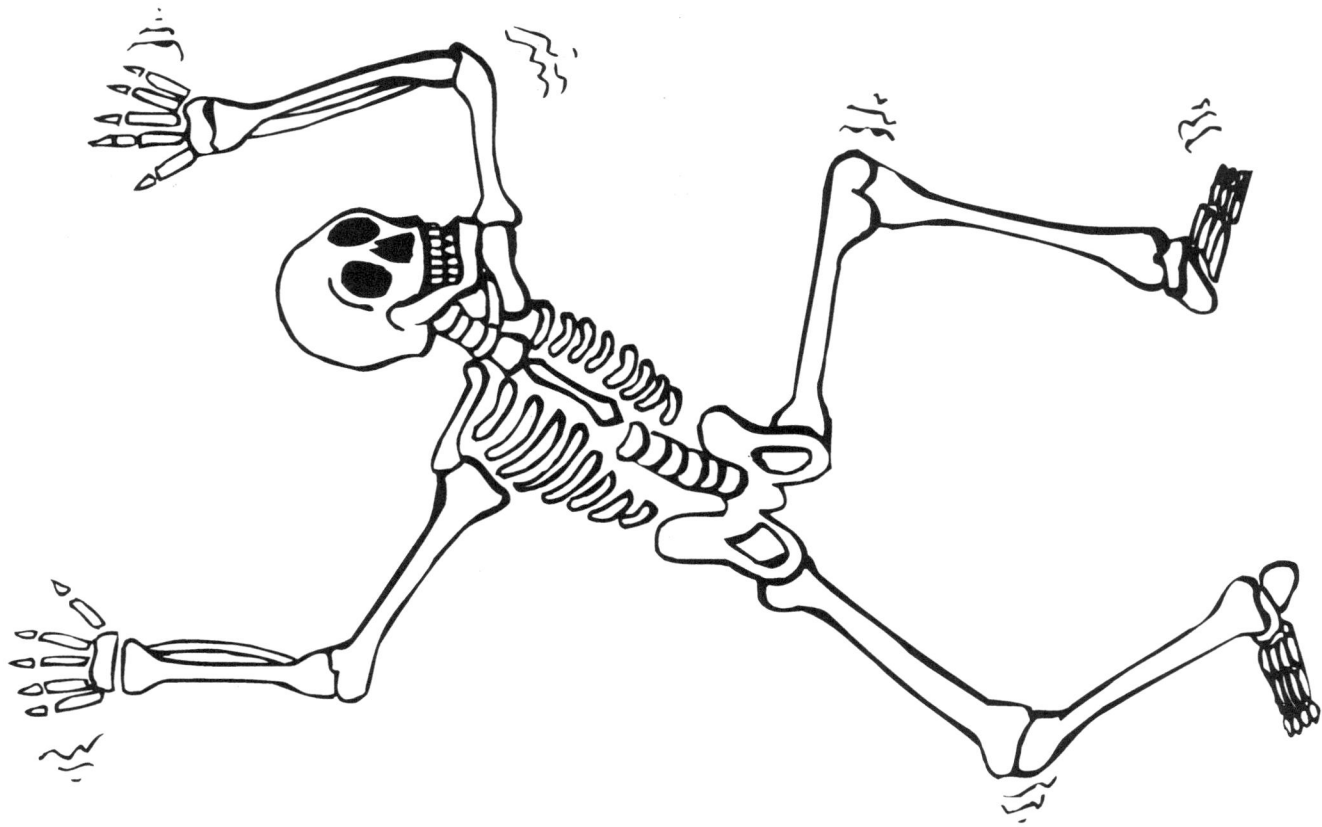

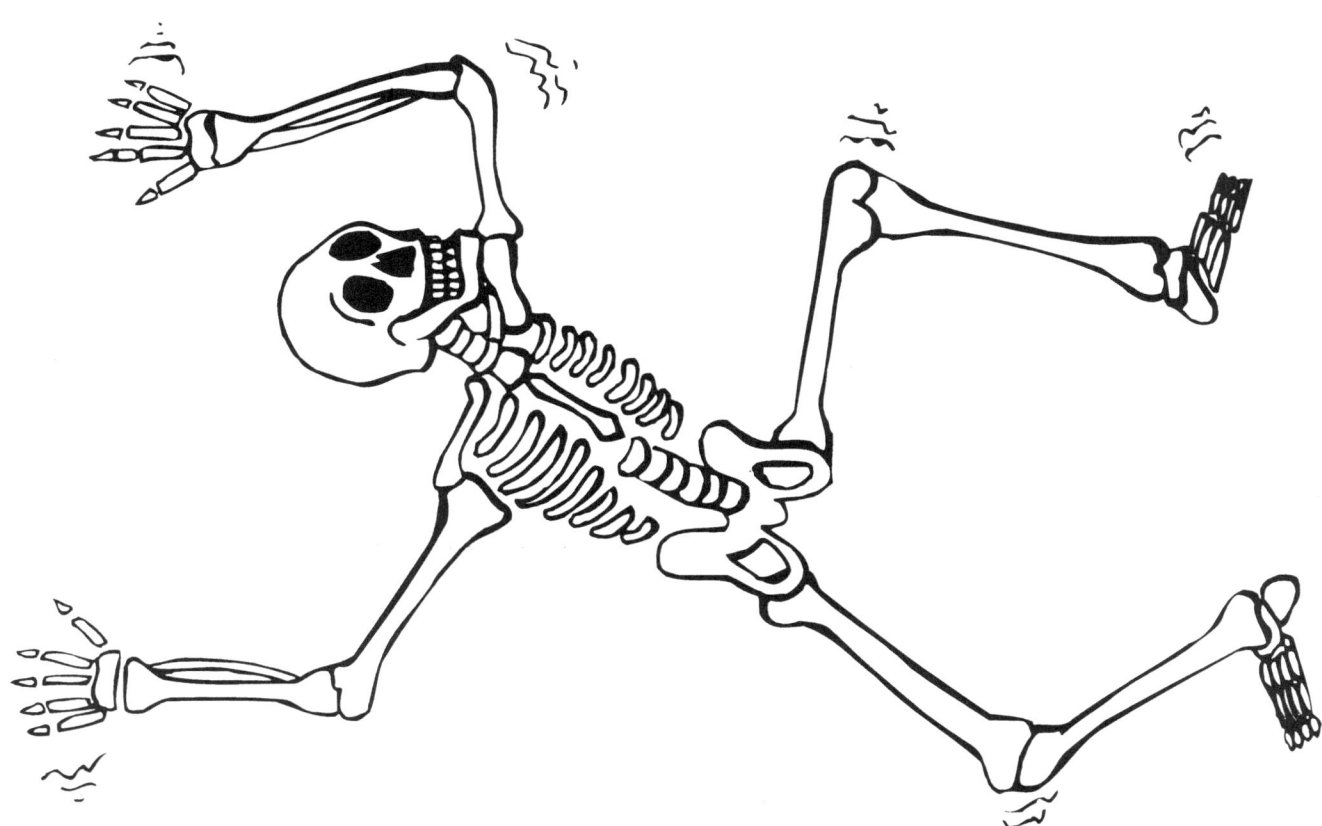

Each pupil has a copy of the picture and the appropriate coloured pencils or crayons.

The teacher reads out each of the instructions twice.

Allow time between each instruction for the pupils to complete the required task.

It does not matter greatly if pupils can see one another's papers, as there are instructions which require different responses from different pupils. You will quickly be able to establish which pupils are following others, and can then arrange to work with those pupils in future exercises.

Instructions

1. Write your name beside the honey-pot.

2. Colour the bear's trousers blue.

3. Put a circle around the bee who wants to share the bear's honey.

4. Colour the bear's body yellow.

5. Draw another two bees who also want to share the honey.

6. Colour the honey-pot green.

7. Find some honey which has spilt on the ground and put a line under it.

8. Think of one other animal which might like to share the bear's honey and draw it in the picture too.

9. Colour the handle of the spoon red.

10. If you think that the bear has a pocket on his trousers, put a large circle right around the picture, but if you think he doesn't, just put a line under your name.

Each pupil has a copy of the picture and the appropriate coloured pencils or crayons.

The teacher reads out each of the instructions twice.

Allow time between each instruction for the pupils to complete the required task.

It does not matter greatly if pupils can see one another's papers, as there are instructions which require different responses from different pupils. You will quickly be able to establish which pupils are following others, and can then arrange to work with those pupils in future exercises.

Instructions

1. Write your name above the puppy's tail.

2. Colour the puppy's ears black.

3. Put a circle around the two flowers which are under the bone.

4. Colour one of the flowers blue and the other three red.

5. Draw another flower behind the puppy and colour it yellow.

6. Colour the puppy's bone brown.

7. Find the lines which show that the puppy is wagging its tail and draw an arrow pointing to them.

8. Think of two different things which fly and draw them in the air above the puppy.

9. Colour the puppy's paws yellow.

10. If the puppy is sitting looking into its kennel, draw the kennel where it must be.

Each pupil has a copy of the picture and the appropriate coloured pencils or crayons.

The teacher reads out each of the instructions twice.

Allow time between each instruction for the pupils to complete the required task.

It does not matter greatly if pupils can see one another's papers, as there are instructions which require different responses from different pupils. You will quickly be able to establish which pupils are following others, and can then arrange to work with those pupils in future exercises.

Instructions

1. Here is a picture of a snowman some children built on a snowy winter's day. Write your name on the snow on the ground.

2. The children used a carrot for the snowman's nose. Colour the carrot the proper colour.

3. Put a circle around the middle button on the snowman's body.

4. The children used buttons for the eyes of the snowman. Colour one button red and the other one blue.

5. The children hung a purse from the hand of the snowman. Draw in the purse.

6. The children used a piece of cloth for the scarf around the snowman's neck. The cloth was red and blue. Colour it in.

7. Find the sign on the snowman's hat and copy what it says onto the sign next to your name.

8. Think of what the snowman's hands are made from and colour them the right colour.

9. Colour the pipe in the snowman's mouth brown.

10. Draw five snowballs on the ground beside the snowman's body.

Listening Comprehension (Lower)

7: Easter Bunny

Each pupil has a copy of the picture and the appropriate coloured pencils or crayons.

The teacher reads out each of the instructions twice.

Allow time between each instruction for the pupils to complete the required task.

It does not matter greatly if pupils can see one another's papers, as there are instructions which require different responses from different pupils. You will quickly be able to establish which pupils are following others, and can then arrange to work with those pupils in future exercises.

Instructions

1. Write your name in the space below the Easter Bunny's foot.

2. Colour the Easter Bunny's ears red.

3. Put a circle around the Easter eggs which are falling out of the Easter Bunny's bowl.

4. Colour the three circles on the bottom of the Easter Bunny's foot in brown.

5. Draw another Easter egg falling out of the Easter Bunny's bowl and decorate it with stripes.

6. There are two eggs in the Easter Bunny's bowl which are decorated with stars. Colour them in yellow.

7. Find the egg in the Easter Bunny's bowl which is decorated with small black dots and colour it in orange.

8. Think of a name for the Easter Bunny and write it above his head.

9. Colour the Easter Bunny's bowl in green and yellow stripes.

10. Draw a large Easter egg for you. Decorate it with circles and squares.

Prim-Ed Publishing

Listening Comprehension (Lower)

Each pupil has a copy of the picture and the appropriate coloured pencils or crayons.

The teacher reads out each of the instructions twice.

Allow time between each instruction for the pupils to complete the required task.

It does not matter greatly if pupils can see one another's papers, as there are instructions which require different responses from different pupils. You will quickly be able to establish which pupils are following others, and can then arrange to work with those pupils in future exercises.

Instructions

1. Write your name above the two balls lying on the ground.

2. The clown is holding an umbrella. Colour it red.

3. Put a circle around the hand the clown is holding nothing in.

4. Colour the monkey's hat green and his stick brown.

5. Draw another ball lying on the ground with the group of three balls.

6. Colour the clown's shoes blue and his hat yellow.

7. Give the clown a big red smiling mouth.

8. Colour the flowers on the clown's pants in red and green.

9. Colour the stripes on the clown's socks orange and the monkey's collar blue.

10. Count the number of buttons on the clown's shirt and write the number above the monkey's hat.

Listening Comprehension (Lower)

Each pupil has a copy of the picture and the appropriate coloured pencils or crayons.

The teacher reads out each of the instructions twice.

Allow time between each instruction for the pupils to complete the required task.

It does not matter greatly if pupils can see one another's papers, as there are instructions which require different responses from different pupils. You will quickly be able to establish which pupils are following others, and can then arrange to work with those pupils in future exercises.

Instructions

1. Write your name above the lid of the pirate's treasure chest.

2. Colour the pirate's sword red.

3. Put a circle around the bag of money lying beside the treasure chest.

4. Colour the pirate's parrot red and green.

5. Draw another pearl necklace lying on the ground beside the treasure chest.

6. The pirate has patches on his pants. Colour one patch blue, one yellow and one orange.

7. Draw a tattoo on the pirate's arm which does not have the parrot sitting on it.

8. Think what sort of ship the pirate would have come on and draw a small picture of it in the background.

9. Colour the gold in yellow and the diamonds in blue.

10. The pirate needs to lock the treasure chest to keep it safe from the other pirates. Draw a picture just above your name of what he will need to do that.

Each pupil has a copy of the picture and the appropriate coloured pencils or crayons.

The teacher reads out each of the instructions twice.

Allow time between each instruction for the pupils to complete the required task.

It does not matter greatly if pupils can see one another's papers, as there are instructions which require different responses from different pupils. You will quickly be able to establish which pupils are following others, and can then arrange to work with those pupils in future exercises.

Instructions

1. Write your name on the side of the bath, just below the soap.

2. Colour the towel hanging over the side of the bath in yellow and red.

3. Put a circle around the toy boat on the side of the bath. Count the number of dots along the side of the boat and write the number beside it.

4. Count how many bubbles are floating in the air above the bath and write the number next to the smallest bubble.

5. Draw another boat in the bath water just behind the girl.

6. Colour the bath duck and the sponge yellow.

7. Find the two bottles of shampoo and colour one green and the other blue.

8. The nearest tap is the hot tap and the far one is the cold tap. Colour the hot tap red and the cold tap blue.

9. Draw a triangle around the largest bubble.

10. Draw four more bubbles above the girl's head.

Prim-Ed Publishing

Each pupil has a copy of the picture and the appropriate coloured pencils or crayons.

The teacher reads out each of the instructions twice.

Allow time between each instruction for the pupils to complete the required task.

It does not matter greatly if pupils can see one another's papers, as there are instructions which require different responses from different pupils. You will quickly be able to establish which pupils are following others, and can then arrange to work with those pupils in future exercises.

Instructions

1. These children have bought some food at the fair. One has an ice-cream, one a hamburger, one a hotdog and one has some fairy floss. Write your name above the head of the girl with the fairy floss.

2. Colour yellow the shirt of the girl with the black hair.

3. Put a circle around the tongue of the girl who is licking her lips.

4. Colour the boy's pocket green and the girl's ribbon red.

5. Draw a ribbon in the hair of the blonde girl with no ribbon.

6. Colour the fairy floss pink and the ice-cream orange.

7. Draw an arrow pointing to the head of the person who has freckles.

8. Draw a cross above the head of the tallest person and another one above the head of the shortest person.

9. Put a zigzag line above the head of the person with the shortest hair and another above the head of the person with the longest hair.

10. Draw a triangle around the one food you would choose out of the four foods shown.

Prim-Ed Publishing

Each pupil has a copy of the picture and the appropriate coloured pencils or crayons.

The teacher reads out each of the instructions twice.

Allow time between each instruction for the pupils to complete the required task.

It does not matter greatly if pupils can see one another's papers, as there are instructions which require different responses from different pupils. You will quickly be able to establish which pupils are following others, and can then arrange to work with those pupils in future exercises.

Instructions

1. Write your name on the sand between the handle of the spade and the bucket.

2. Colour one feather green and the other one red.

3. Put a square around the snail shell which has been used to help decorate the sandcastle.

4. Colour the sails of one boat orange and the sails of the other red.

5. Draw another sailboat on the water.

6. Colour purple the starfish design on the side of the bucket.

7. Draw a line going from one of the seagulls, down around the smallest cloud and back up to the other seagull.

8. The flag should have three stars on it. Draw them there.

9. Colour brown the fan shell and the large stone near the spade.

10. If you think that the picture is about daytime, colour the stick holding the flag brown. If you think that the picture is about night-time, colour the spade red.

Listening Comprehension (Lower)

Prim-Ed Publishing

My Listening Success Graph

Name: . . . .

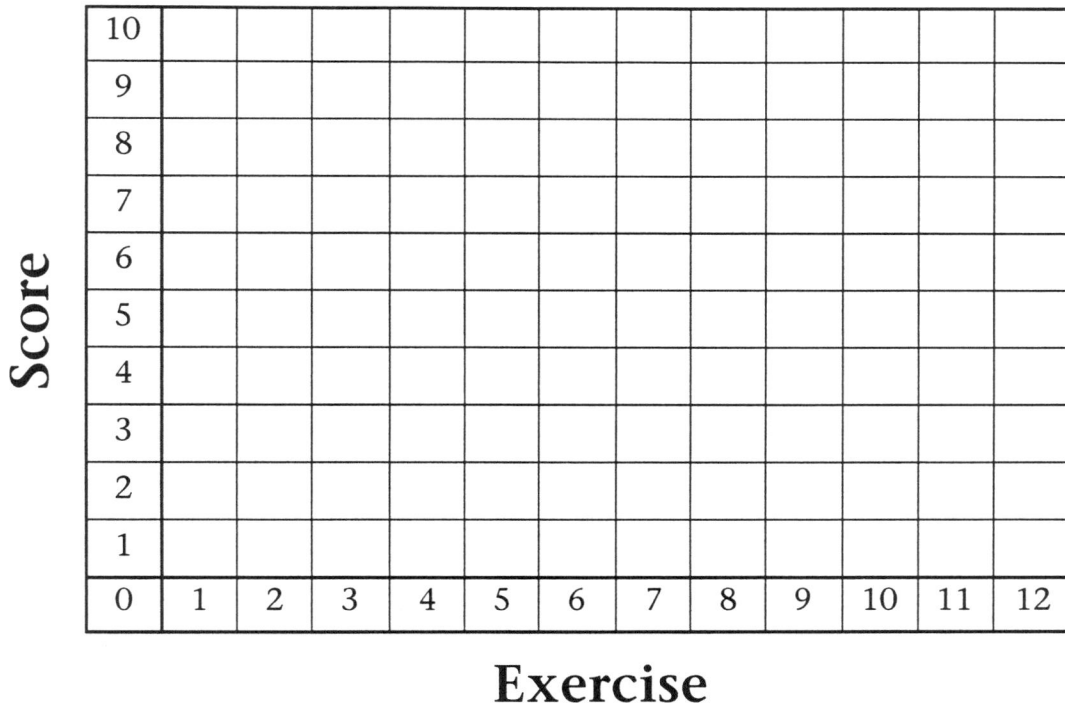

Score

Exercise

My Listening Success Graph

Name: . . . .

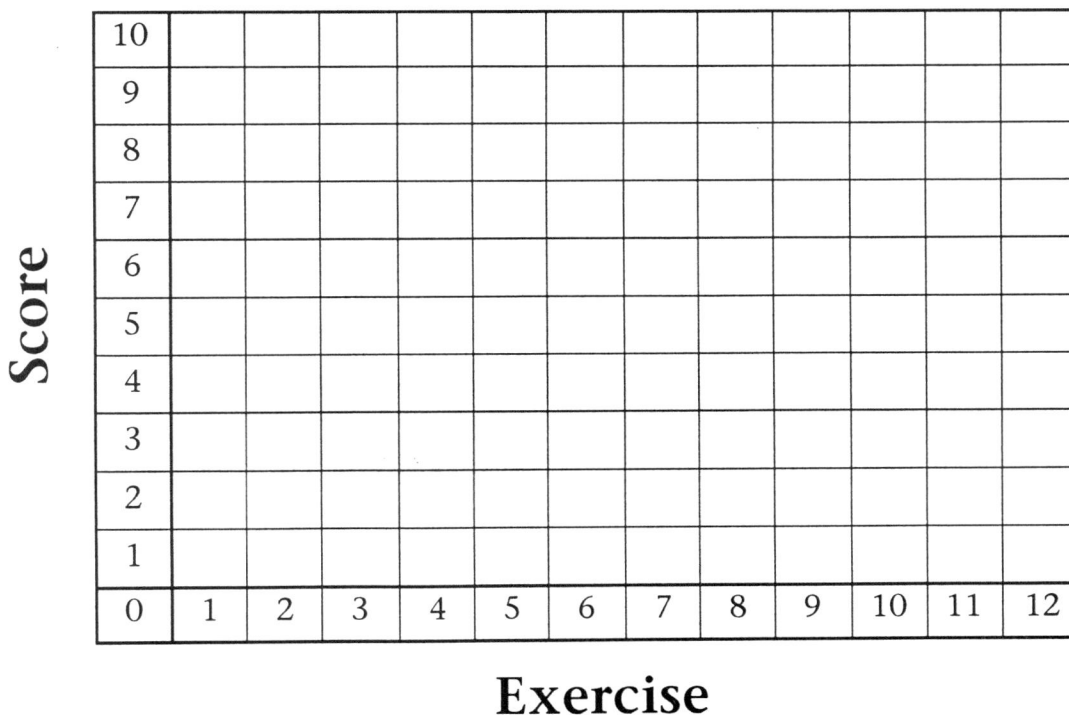

Score

Exercise

Prim-Ed Publishing